Edmund Dulac

BIRTHDAY
BOOK

BIRTHDAY
BOOK

HODDER AND STOUGHTON

LONDON SYDNEY AUCKLAND TORONTO

Edmund Dulac's life spanned two world wars and almost seven decades. He was born on October 22nd 1882 at Toulouse. Throughout his childhood he was surrounded by paintings; his father, a commercial traveller for a textile firm, was also a keen collector of old paintings which he bought, restored and sometimes sold. As a child, Edmund Dulac already showed the talent for drawing which was to gain him the reputation of one of the greatest illustrators of the early twentieth century.

He had a comfortable upbringing, living with his parents and grandmother in the large house on the Rue de Montaudron where he had been born. At the age of eight he was enrolled at the Petit Lycée in Toulouse, where he stayed until he had gained his Baccalauréat. At fourteen he was painting with skill and delicacy – a water-colour of his grandmother, painted at that age, shows the control of colour and form which characterises his later work. He kept innumerable sketch-books which he filled with drawings of the streets and alleyways of Toulouse and the bustling life around him.

After he had passed his Baccalauréat he joined the Department of Law at Toulouse University. His parents, although aware of their son's artistic talents, felt that he would need a career which would provide stability. Dulac still continued to draw and paint and attended classes at the Ecole des Beaux Arts.

He gained an intermediate degree of Litt. Ph.B. and, having satisfied his parent's wishes, immediately left university to attend art school full time. Perhaps one of the factors which encouraged him to take this step was the fact that the Toulouse *Télégramme* had already used one of his designs for the cover of their Christmas number.

At this time, Dulac's uncle, who traded in 'Fancy Goods' was importing decorative work from the East; Dulac saw, and was very influenced by, some of the Japanese wood-block prints that his uncle was selling. His drawings took on a new dimension: instead of the highly realistic style he had been using, he began to incorporate into his work a more sinuous quality, a feeling for the 'design' of a picture, rather than the straightforward depiction of what he saw. This was a trait that became more and more dominant in his work as his style developed. While Dulac was attending the Ecole des Beaux Arts he moved out of his parents' house and into rooms which he shared with a fellow student — Emile Rixens, a man who was to remain a close friend for the rest of his life. It was at this time that Dulac began to learn English, paying for his lessons by painting portraits of his tutor and family. He became such an anglophile that he was affectionately known among the students as 'L'anglais'.

During his three years at the art school in Toulouse, Dulac achieved several successes, winning the Grand Prix twice (the annual prize given by the Ecole des Beaux Arts) and the Petit Prix once. He was also chosen to illuminate a parchment menu given to the President of France after an official dinner held in Toulouse.

In 1903 he won a scholarship to the Académie Julien, an independent art school in Paris. Alphonse Mucha and Will Rothenstein had studied there and Kay Nielsen was to attend later. To his horror he found that far from being allowed to develop his own style, he was required to make interminable copies of epic paintings and drawings from plaster casts. His tutor, Jean Paul Laurens, had studied and taught at Toulouse and was very traditional in his approach to art. Dulac hated the few months he attended the Académie Julien and finally left. He must have been bitterly disappointed to find no outlet for his expanding awareness of technique and form.

In 1903, while on holiday in Biarritz, he met Alice May de Marini, an American; she was thirteen years older than him and the daughter of Italian-American parents. After a whirlwind courtship they were married in December of that year. Sadly, the marriage was not a success and they parted soon after. Dulac returned to Toulouse to live with his parents.

He had entered several pictures for the Paris Salon Spring Exhibition and one of these, a portrait of his grandmother, painted in 1902, was accepted. In 1904 he at last visited England. He was looking for work from English publishers and was commissioned by J M Dent to produce 60 water-colours to illustrate a collection of the Brontë novels. The first twelve were produced within three months and Dulac went on to illustrate the complete collection. These were received favourably by the critics, and in the same year he once again had a picture exhibited at the Paris Salon — a portrait of an English flower-seller. His work came to the attention of the editors of the *Pall Mall* magazine, and, encouraged by this success he returned to England in 1905 to try and earn his living. On his return to England he lived in rented rooms at 16a Aubrey Walk, Holland Park, London (a previous tenant had been John Galsworthy); he joined the London Sketch Club and became very interested in book design and illustration.

At this time, illustrated books had reached a level of excellence never achieved before; perhaps due to a technique of colour printing developed by Carl Hentschel which allowed the reproduction of colour plates with real accuracy. This required heavy, glazed paper, and the plates had to be inserted into the book by hand; consequently the borders to the plates, the general design of the books and the opportunity to experiment with type styles and format offered a new field to illustrators. The borders around the colour plates in this book are taken from original Dulac designs.

In 1906 Edmund Dulac took his portfolio to the Leicester Galleries. Ernest Brown, co-owner of the galleries, was very impressed with Dulac's work and commissioned him to illustrate a new project – *The Arabian Nights*. Dulac was to receive a flat fee in exchange for the original illustrations and the copyright. The Leicester Galleries sold the rights to Hodder and Stoughton who published the book and founded a partnership that was to continue for more than a decade.

Perhaps the most prestigious illustrator of the era was Arthur Rackham and publishers vied with each other to commission him to illustrate their books. Heinemann and Hodder and Stoughton had both approached Rackham to illustrate a Christmas Gift Book, Heinemann had won. Hodder and Stoughton then took the bold step of using a virtually unknown illustrator for their Gift Book; this young man was Edmund Dulac.

In 1907 *The Arabian Nights* was published: the Leicester Galleries exhibited the original illustrations simultaneously and they were all sold before the general public were able to see the exhibition. The book was a tremendous success and Hodder and Stoughton immediately commissioned Dulac to do their next Christmas Gift Book. The Leicester Galleries and Hodder and Stoughton offered Dulac a contract to do one book a year for them, the French rights being sold to Henry Piazza in Paris.

In 1908 Dulac's wife sued him for divorce for desertion and the petition was successful. Dulac was now free and living in England where his work was truly appreciated. In the same year *The Tempest*, Hodder and Stoughton's Christmas Gift Book, was published and took the publishing world by storm. It was so successful that a calendar incorporating the illustrations was produced later that year. Dulac was also working on illustrations for the *Pall Mall* magazine and for *L'Illustration*, a magazine published in France by Henry Piazza and had his own work published by Frederick Warne – *Lyrics Pathetic and Humorous from A to Z*. He was also illustrating the Christmas Gift Book for 1909, *The Rubaiyat of Omar Khayyam*. In this year of success Dulac met Elsa Arnalice Bignardi at a concert and had fell in love with her.

They lived together for two years and married at the Marylebone Registry Office in April 1911, with Ernest Brown of the Leicester Galleries as their witness.

The Gift Book for 1910 was *The Sleeping Beauty and Other Fairy Stories* and Dulac's new wife was immortalised as the heroine of the 'Sleeping Beauty', 'Beauty and the Beast' and 'Bluebeard'. The model for 'Cinderella' was Lea Rixens, the young wife of Emile Rixens. The next year Dulac started work on the Hodder and Stoughton Gift Book for 1911 – *Stories from Hans Andersen* – and in March heard that he had been awarded two gold medals at the Barcelona International Exhibition; these were given for the originals of the Hans Andersen Gift Book as well as four illustrations for the Christmas edition of *L'Illustration*. In February 1912 he became a naturalised British citizen.

Edmund Dulac was now firmly established as one of the leading illustrators of his time. Always looking for new outlets for his talent he was delighted to be commissioned to design costumes and sets for a ballet which was to be set to music by Debussy; sadly the ballet was never completed. In 1912 Dulac and Elsa moved into 72 Ladbroke Grove, one of a group of studios built on to existing houses by Edmund Davis. Here they met W B Yeats, Charles Shannon and Charles Ricketts, among many writers, poets and artists who were to become lifelong friends.

The Gift Book for 1912 was *The Bells*, a collection of Edgar Allen Poe's poems. This sombre work, illustrated by 28 watercolours, was received coolly by the critics. In 1913, Dulac was working on *Princess Badoura*, and was beginning to chafe under the constraint that his success had brought. Dulac was always looking for new ideas and new techniques of illustration. His work was very popular but any departure from his recognised style was frowned upon. Dulac was beginning to be influenced by Persian and Chinese art and wished to incorporate this into his

10

illustrations. *Sinbad the Sailor and Other Stories from the Arabian Nights* shows this influence strongly. In 1914, when war was declared, Dulac was asked to create charity stamps and inexpensive gift books, the *Princess Mary Gift Book* and *King Albert's Book* were published, both of which contained illustrations by Dulac. He was also working on caricatures, a skill which he had used rarely before. In 1915 the *Daily Telegraph* asked Dulac to compile a picture book for the French Red Cross. This was a great honour, and showed how highly acclaimed Dulac was. During the war Dulac worked constantly on posters, caricatures and books, including the illustrations for Queen Marie of Roumania's book *The Dreamer of Dreams*.

In 1915 Dulac began work on *Edmund Dulac's Fairy Book*, a compilation of fairy tales of the Allied Nations; this book combined a great range of styles and is perhaps the best example of Dulac's versatility. He was also working on the costumes for the stage version of 'Phoebus and Pan' which was to be performed by the newly formed Beecham Opera Company. The costumes and sets were stupendous and despite problems about payment Dulac enjoyed the challenge that this offered.

The following year, while he was working on the *Fairy Book*, W B Yeats asked Dulac to collaborate with him on a series of plays based on the Japanese 'Noh' Theatre. Dulac not only designed the sets and costumes, but also wrote and played the flute music which accompanied the actors. This versatility caused him great amusement some years later when Puccini, having heard that Dulac could write passably 'Chinese' music asked him to send him some tunes which could be used in Turandot; Dulac, thinking that Puccini was only being polite, ignored the request, only to receive a letter, asking him once more to send some tunes. Dulac did, and Puccini based several arias on Dulac's themes.

The final gift book for Hodder and Stoughton was *Tanglewood*

Tales; Dulac started on it in 1916 but it was not published until 1918 because of the shortage of paper after the war. In 1917, after witnessing terrible air raids on London, Dulac and Elsa moved to 'Dewlands' at Cranleigh in Surrey; the war and the air raids had had a dreadful effect on Elsa and she began to have hallucinations and bouts of severe depression. Elsa's mother came to live with them to look after her daughter. After the armistice the Dulacs returned to Ladbroke Grove where Dulac, having no large publishing contracts had to exist by painting portraits. In 1918 C B Cochran asked Dulac to design the costume and sets for the musical version of 'Cyrano De Bergerac'. Dulac's designs were magnificent, although he came to dislike the leading actor Robert Lorraine intensely and was very unhappy working with him.

In February of 1919 Dulac began to work for *The Outlook* as their resident cartoonist, this was to last for two years until the newspaper had to close. Another facet of Dulac's versatility surfaced at this time; he began to design character dolls — tiny models, exact in every detail and wickedly witty in their depiction of the character they represented.

In 1919 the Dulacs moved to a larger studio on the opposite side of Ladbroke Road. Dulac was having financial difficulties and Elsa was becoming more and more unwell. Edmund Dulac had formed a close friendship with Frederick McCurdy Atkinson over the last few years, and met a protegée of his — Helen Beauclerk. This was to be a fateful meeting.

Dulac finished his final gift book in 1919. This was not published by Hodder and Stoughton, but by James Nisbet. *The Pearl* contains some of Dulac's finest work; delicate, complicated and innovative, it shows clearly how Dulac had mastered the techniques he had learned over the years he had been illustrating. The De Luxe edition sold out instantly but the unsigned edition was remaindered.

The next few years were lean ones for the Dulacs. There was little work in British publishing although the *American Weekly* regularly commissioned him to do illustrations. In 1922, Dulac worked with C B Cochran again, but was not happy with the result. Although he was still making ends meet by doing portraits he had only one real triumph to console him. He was asked to design two rooms for The Queen's Dolls' House; he designed the Queen's Sitting Room and the Day Nursery, even going so far as to make a small character doll of Queen Victoria which he ceremonially seated in the lavatory (this was removed later).

In 1923 Elsa and Edmund Dulac separated and Helen Beauclerk moved into Ladbroke Road with Dulac. Although he was emotionally happy he still had serious money worries and hated having to work for the *American Weekly* which he thought was over-sensational. He illustrated Helen's book *The Green Lacquer Pavilion* and this was very favourably received. In 1927 Ernest Benn commissioned Dulac to illustrate *Treasure Island*. This became Dulac's favourite book, and he maintained that they were the only illustrations he would never try to change. The following year he illustrated *The Fairy Garland* for Cassell and in 1929 supervised the decorations for the Chelsea Arts Ball, a sensational arrangement that was based on Aladdin's cave. He also designed a room for the Daily Mail Ideal Home Exhibition and had some of his furniture designs copied for use aboard the Canadian Pacific liner *The Empress of Britain*.

The 1930s showed another facet of Dulac's talents. He began to design medals and stamps. With his attention to detail and accuracy of line, Dulac was eminently suited to this. These were difficult years for Dulac. There was little work available and even though he received commissions from the Royal Mint to design medals and coins these were poorly paid. Dulac designed the stamps for the coronation of King George VI and during the Second World War designed stamps and banknotes for the exiled

French and Belgian governments. In 1949 he had a serious heart attack and was ill for several months. He recovered and designed the stamps for Queen Elizabeth II's coronation.

On the 25th of May 1953 Edmund Dulac died after a heart attack which was thought to have been brought on by demonstrating flamenco dancing to a friend. He had always been passionately interested in flamenco and used to practise and dance regularly. If this is true it seems quite typical of Dulac, for he was always a man who involved himself thoroughly in everything he did.

He left behind him a series of books and illustrations which will give pleasure to generations of children and adults and he founded a tradition in illustration that still touches artists today.

JANUARY

Looking forward into an empty year
strikes one with a certain awe,
because one finds therein no recognition.
The years behind have a friendly aspect,
and they are warmed by the fires
we have kindled.

ALEXANDER SMITH

1

Let us all be happy,
and live within our means,
even if we have to borrow
to do it with.
ARTEMUS WARD

2

A little sincerity
is a dangerous thing,
and a great deal of it
is absolutely fatal.
OSCAR WILDE

3

The young ladies entered
the ballroom in the full fervour
of sisterly animosity.
ROBERT SMITH SURTEES

4

I never read a book before
reviewing it;
it prejudices a man so.
REV. SIDNEY SMITH

5

It takes two to speak the truth —
one to speak and one to hear.
HENRY DAVID THOREAU

6

Soap and education are not as
sudden as a massacre,
but they are more deadly
in the long run.
MARK TWAIN

7

In my early years I read very hard.
It is a sad reflection,
but a true one, that I knew almost
as much at eighteen as I do now.
SAMUEL JOHNSON

8

Give me books, fruit,
french wine and fine weather
and a little music out of doors,
played by somebody I do not know.
JOHN KEATS

The angels all were singing out of tune,
And hoarse with having little else to do,
Excepting to wind up the sun and moon,
Or curb a runaway young star or two.
LORD BYRON

9

Unlike grownups, children have
little need to deceive themselves.
GOETHE

10

To have a good enemy,
choose a friend:
He knows where to strike.
DIANE DE POITIERS

11

'Presents,' I often say,
'endear Absents.'
CHARLES LAMB

12

Anything awful makes me laugh.
I misbehaved once at a funeral.
CHARLES LAMB

13

Remember that the most
beautiful things in the world
are the most useless;
peacocks and lilies for instance.
JOHN RUSKIN

14

In baiting a mousetrap with cheese,
always leave room for the mouse.
SAKI

15

If one is really a superior person,
the fact is likely to leak out
without too much assistance.
JOHN ANDREW HOLMES

16

We are always
getting ready to live,
but never living.
EMERSON

17

The unknown always
passes for the marvellous.
TACITUS

18

Grieve not that men
do not know you, rather grieve
that you do not know men.
CONFUCIUS

19

The majority of husbands
remind me of an orangutan
trying to play the violin.
HONORE DE BALZAC

20

Titles are but nicknames,
and every nickname is a title.
THOMAS PAINE

I remember the black wharves and the slips,
and the sea-tides tossing free —
And Spanish sailors with bearded lips,
And the beauty and mystery of the ships,
And the magic of the sea.
HENRY WADSWORTH LONGFELLOW

21

There is no good
in arguing with the inevitable.
The only argument available
with an east wind
is to put on your overcoat.
JAMES RUSSELL LOWELL

22

At night there is no such thing
as an ugly woman.
OVID

23

To be nobly wrong is more manly
than to be meanly right.
THOMAS PAINE

24

Nothing will ever be attempted,
if all possible objections
must first be overcome.
SAMUEL JOHNSON

25

Go and wake up your luck.
PERSIAN PROVERB

26

We brought nothing into this world,
and it is certain we can carry
nothing out.
THE BIBLE.   1 TIMOTHY 6:7

27

Society is now one polished horde,
Formed of two mighty tribes,
The Bores and Bored.
LORD BYRON

28

Brevity is very good,
When we are,
or are not understood.
SAMUEL BUTLER

29

Wit is so shining a quality
that everybody admires it;
most people aim at it,
all people fear it,
and few love it except in
themselves.
LORD CHESTERFIELD

30

If a handsome woman allows
that another woman is beautiful,
we may safely conclude that she
excels her.
LA BRUYERE

31

Youth is the time to go
flashing from one end of the world
to the other,
both in the mind and body.
ROBERT LOUIS STEVENSON

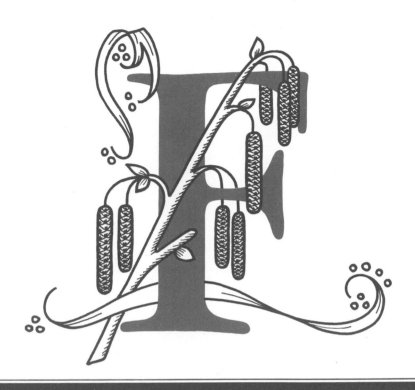

FEBRUARY

There is no more lovely,
friendly and charming relationship,
communion or company than
a good marriage.
MARTIN LUTHER

1

Man is the only animal that
blushes.
Or needs to.
MARK TWAIN

2

Poverty is no disgrace to a man,
but it is confoundedly
inconvenient.
REV. SIDNEY SMITH

3

The axis of the earth sticks out
visibly through the centre
of each and every town or city.
OLIVER WENDELL HOLMES

4

The language of friendship is
not words but meanings.
THOREAU

5

Let us be of good cheer, however,
remembering that the misfortunes
hardest to bear are those
which never come.
JAMES RUSSELL LOWELL

6

Man, n. An animal so lost in
rapturous contemplation of
what he thinks he is
as to overlook
what he indubitably ought to be.
AMBROSE BIERCE

7

Would that I could discover truth
as easily as I can uncover
falsehood.
CICERO

8

How much of human life is
lost in waiting.
EMERSON

There is not so variable a thing in nature
as a lady's headdress: within my own memory
I have known it rise and fall above thirty degrees.
JOSEPH ADDISON

9

Sciences may be learned by rote,
but wisdom not.
LAURENCE STERNE

10

The well-bred contradict
other people.
The wise contradict themselves.
OSCAR WILDE

11

Shall I be remembered after death?
I sometimes think and hope so.
But I trust I may not be found out
before my death.
SAMUEL BUTLER

12

A moment's insight is sometimes
worth a life's experience.
OLIVER WENDELL HOLMES

13

Better to turn back
than to lose your way.
RUSSIAN PROVERB

14

The remedy for all blunders,
the cure of blindness,
the cure of crime, is love.
EMERSON

15

Happiness depends as Nature shows,
Less on exterior things than most
suppose.
WILLIAM COWPER

16

Illusory joy is often worth more
than genuine sorrow.
DESCARTES

17

A promise is binding
in the inverse ratio
of the numbers to whom it is made.
THOMAS DE QUINCEY

18

Without wearing any mask
that we are conscious of,
we have a special face for each
friend.
OLIVER WENDELL HOLMES SNR.

19

Charm: that quality in others of
making us more satisfied with
ourselves.
HENRI FREDERIC AMIEL

20

People seem not to see
that their opinion of the world
is also a confession of character.
EMERSON

It is not in the storm nor in the strife
We feel benumbed, and wish to be no more,
But in the after-silence on the shore,
When all is lost, except a little life.
LORD BYRON

21

Corporeal charms may indeed
gain admirers, but there must be
mental ones to retain them.
CHARLES CALEB COLTON

22

He's my friend that speaks well of
me behind my back.
THOMAS FULLER

23

All who joy would win
Must share it,
Happiness was born a twin.
LORD BYRON

24

Vanity is truly the motive-power
that moves humanity,
and it is flattery that
greases the wheels.
JEROME K JEROME

25

A man who makes no mistakes
does not usually make anything.
WILLIAM CONNER MAGEE

26

The difference between Talent
and Genius is, that Talent says
things he has heard but once,
and Genius says things which he has
never heard.
EMERSON

27

Half our mistakes in life arise
from feeling where we ought to
think, and thinking
where we ought to feel.
JOHN CHURTON COLLINS

28

To burn always with this hard,
gemlike flame, to maintain this
ecstacy, is success in life.
WALTER PATER

29

Strange to see how a good dinner
and feasting reconciles everybody.
SAMUEL PEPYS

MARCH

. . . in truth the months which should be made
to look gloomy in England are March and April.
Let no man boast himself
that he has got through the perils of winter
till at least the seventh of May.

ANTHONY TROLLOPE

1

Sweet is the scene where
genial plays,
The pleasing game
of interchanging praise.
OLIVER WENDELL HOLMES

2

I am, indeed a king,
because I know how to rule myself.
PIETRO ARETINO

3

The years that a woman subtracts
from her age are not lost. They
are added to other women's.
DIANE DE POITIERS

4

A man who is master of himself
can end a sorrow
as easily as he can invent
a pleasure.
OSCAR WILDE

5

When angry, count a hundred;
when very angry, swear.
MARK TWAIN

6

All the world is odd save thee and
me, and even thou
art a little queer.
ROBERT OWEN

7

Men are generally more careful
of the breed of their horses and
dogs than of their children.
WILLIAM PENN

8

Civility cost nothing
and buys everything.
LADY MARY WORTLEY MONTAGU

Nature's great masterpiece, an elephant,
The only great harmless thing . . .
JOHN DONNE

9

He who praises everybody
praises nobody.
SAMUEL JOHNSON

10

Ask yourself whether you are happy,
and you cease to be so.
JOHN STUART MILL

11

There is but one step
from the sublime to the ridiculous.
NAPOLEON I

12

How few of his friend's houses
would a man choose to be at
when he is sick.
SAMUEL JOHNSON

13

No more things should be
presumed to exist than are
absolutely necessary.
WILLIAM OCCAM

14

The devil's most devilish
when respectable.
ELIZABETH BARRET BROWNING

15

All intellectual improvement arises
from leisure.
SAMUEL JOHNSON

16

Reading is to the mind
what exercise is to the body.
SIR RICHARD STEELE

17

Our life is frittered away by
detail . . .
simplify, simplify.
HENRY DAVID THOREAU

18

More people are flattered into
virtue than bullied out of vice.
ROBERT SMITH SURTEES

19

Reading is sometimes an ingenious
device for avoiding thought.
SAMUEL JOHNSON

20

Love is not love which alters when
it alteration finds.
WILLIAM SHAKESPEARE

Women are the decorative sex,
They never have anything to say,
but they say it charmingly.
OSCAR WILDE

21

The reason why lovers are never
weary of one another is this:
they are always talking of
themselves.
LA ROCHEFOUCAULD

22

Some circumstantial evidence is
very strong, as when you find a
trout in the milk.
HENRY DAVID THOREAU

23

It matters not how a man dies,
but how he lives. The act of dying
is not of importance,
it lasts so short a time.
SAMUEL JOHNSON

24

An acquaintance that begins
with a compliment is sure
to develop into a real friendship.
OSCAR WILDE

25

Take the flower and turn the hour,
and kiss your love again.
RUDYARD KIPLING

26

To most men, experience is like
the stern lights of a ship, which
illuminate only the track it has
passed.
SAMUEL TAYLOR COLERIDGE

27

Beware of telling
an improbable truth.
DR THOMAS FULLER

28

There is no bore
like a clever bore.
SAMUEL BUTLER II

29

People count up the faults of those
who are keeping them waiting.
FRENCH PROVERB

30

A wise man will live as much
within his wit as his income.
LORD CHESTERFIELD

31

A man who lives free from folly
is not as wise as he thinks.
LA ROCHEFOUCAULD

APRIL

When I arose and saw the dawn
　　　I sighed for thee;
When light rode high and the dew was gone,
And noon lay heavy on flower and tree,
And the weary day turned to his rest,
Lingering like an unloved guest,
　　　I sighed for thee.

PERCY BYSSHE SHELLEY

1

Be wise with speed;
a fool at forty
is a fool indeed.
EDWARD YOUNG

2

Let me smile with the wise
and feed with the rich.
SAMUEL JOHNSON

3

Everyone is more or less mad
on one point.
RUDYARD KIPLING

4

It's not that age brings
childhood back again,
Age merely shows us
what children we remain.
GOETHE

5

Most people die of a sort of
creeping common sense,
and discover when it is too late
that the only things one never
regrets are one's mistakes.
OSCAR WILDE

6

We must like what we have
when we do not have what we like.
ROGER DE BUSSY RABUTIN

7

You have not converted a man
because you have silenced him.
JOHN MORLEY

8

He who can take no interest
in what is small will take
false interest in what is great.
JOHN RUSKIN

She was not quite what you would call refined.
She was not quite what you would call unrefined.
She was the kind of person that keeps a parrot
MARK TWAIN

9

Nature uses as little as
possible of anything.
JOHANNES KEPLER

10

Life is the art of drawing
sufficient conclusions
from insufficient premises.
SAMUEL BUTLER II

11

Diogenes struck the father
when the son swore.
ROBERT BURTON

12

'Tis healthy to be sick sometimes.
THOREAU

13

Truth generally is kindness, but
where the two diverge and collide,
kindness should override truth.
SAMUEL BUTLER II

14

No man is rich enough
to buy back his past.
OSCAR WILDE

15

It is harder to hide feelings we
have than to feign those we lack:
LA ROCHEFOUCAULD

16

Experience is the name
everyone gives to his mistakes.
OSCAR WILDE

17

Power is not revealed by
striking hard or often,
but by striking true.
HONORE DE BALZAC

18

A man is in general better pleased
when he has a good dinner upon his
table than when his wife talks
Greek.
DR JOHNSON

19

Visits always give pleasure —
if not the arrival,
the departure.
PORTUGUESE PROVERB

20

I hate war: it ruins conversation.
BERNARD DE FONTENELLE

My soul is an enchanted boat,
Which, like a sleeping swan, doth float
Upon the silver waves of thy sweet singing.
PERCY BYSSHE SHELLEY

21

No one ever keeps a secret
so well as a child.
VICTOR HUGO

22

Friendship is like money,
easier made than kept.
SAMUEL BUTLER II

23

Friendship is love
without his wings.
LORD BYRON

24

However rare true love may be,
it is less so than true friendship.
LA ROCHEFOUCAULD

25

There is less harm to be suffered
in being mad among madmen
than in being sane all by oneself.
DENIS DIDEROT

26

It is not from reason and
prudence that people marry,
but from inclination.
SAMUEL JOHNSON

27

There is no gathering the rose
without being pricked by the
thorns.
FABLES OF BIDPAI

28

Old age is not a total misery.
Experience helps.
EURIPIDES

29

We can outrun the wind and the
storm but we cannot outrun
the Demon of Hurry.
JOHN BURROUGHS

30

Those that fly may fight again,
Which he can never do that's slain.
Hence timely running's no mean part
Of conduct in the martial art.
SAMUEL BUTLER

MAY

All Nature seems at work. Slugs leave their lair —
The bees are stirring — birds are on the wing —
And Winter, slumbering in the open air,
Wears on his smiling face a dream of Spring.
SAMUEL TAYLOR COLERIDGE

1

You never know what is enough
unless you know what is
more than enough.
WILLIAM BLAKE

2

Nature never breaks her own laws.
LEONARDO DA VINCI

3

A host is like a general:
it takes a mishap to reveal
his genius.
HORACE

4

Forsake not an old friend,
for a new one does not
compare with him.
THE BIBLE
ECCLESIASTICUS 9:10

5

Better mad with the rest
of the world than wise alone.
BALTASAR GRACIAN

6

A friend is a person
with whom I may be sincere.
Before him I may think aloud.
EMERSON

7

I have often regretted my speech,
but never my silences.
PUBLILIUS SYRUS

8

Scratching is one of
nature's gratifications,
and nearest at hand.
MONTAIGNE

There is nothing that disgusts
a man like getting beaten
at chess by a woman.
CHARLES DUDLEY WARNER

9

Evidence of trust begets trust,
and love is reciprocated by love.
PLUTARCH

10

We are so happy to advise others
that occasionally we even do it
in their interest.
JULES RENARD

11

Too much rigidity on the part of
teachers should be followed by a
brisk spirit of insubordination on
the part of the taught.
AGNES REPPLIER

12

If the blind lead the blind,
both fall in the ditch.
ANGLO-SAXON PROVERB

13

Pigs may fly;
but they are very unlikely birds.
E. P. HOOD

14

Women and music
should never be dated.
OLIVER GOLDSMITH

15

Wise men change their minds,
fools never.
MABBE

16

Wishes can never fill a sack.
ITALIAN PROVERB

17

Two things a man should never
be angry at, what he can help,
and what he cannot help.
JAMES KELLY

18

Time and thinking
tame the strongest grief.
A. HENDERSON

19

Things which are non-apparent
must be treated as non-existent.
ALEX MACLAREN

20

Measurement of life should be
proportioned rather to the
intensity of the experience
than to its actual length.
THOMAS HARDY

Everyone carries his own inch-rule of taste,
and amuses himself by applying it, triumphantly,
wherever he travels.
HENRY ADAMS

21

Love is the admiration and
cherishing of the amiable qualities
of the beloved person, upon the
condition of yourself being the
object of their action.
SAMUEL TAYLOR COLERIDGE

22

They do not love
that do not show their love.
WILLIAM SHAKESPEARE

23

Mankind are earthen jugs
with spirits in them.
NATHANIEL HAWTHORNE

24

I'm not denyin' the women are
foolish: God Almighty made 'em to
match the man.
GEORGE ELIOT

25

I have no malice
in my heart at all,
but I much prefer people
who like me, to people who don't.
RICHARD GRIMES

26

Distance has the same effect
on the mind as on the eye.
SAMUEL JOHNSON

27

Few people desire the pleasures
that they are free to take.
OVID

28

The difference between
gossip and philosophy lies only
in one's way of taking a fact.
OLIVER WENDELL HOLMES JNR.

29

Nothing is an unmixed blessing.
HORACE

30

He is well paid that is
well satisfied.
SHAKESPEARE

31

A thing well said will be wit
in all languages.
JOHN DRYDEN

JUNE

Their meetings made December June,
Their every parting was to die.
ALFRED, LORD TENNYSON

1

Between friends there is
no need of justice.
ARISTOTLE

2

Many a time the thing left silent
makes for happiness.
PINDAR

3

When there is no peril in the
fight, there is no glory in the
triumph.
PIERRE CORNEILLE

4

I could never look long upon a
monkey, without very mortifying
reflections.
WILLIAM CONGREVE

5

The ear of jealousy heareth all
things.
THE BIBLE
WISDOM OF SOLOMON 1:10

6

Resolve to be thyself: and know,
that he who finds himself,
loses his misery.
MATTHEW ARNOLD

7

No, there's nothing half so sweet
in life as love's young dream.
THOMAS MOORE

8

Secrets with girls, like loaded
guns with boys,
Are never valued till
they make a noise.
GEORGE CRABBE

Her eyes the glow-worm lend thee,
The shooting stars attend thee;
And the elves also,
Whose little eyes glow
Like the sparks of fire attend thee.
ROBERT HERRICK

9

Heat not a furnace for your foe so
hot, that it doth singe yourself.
WILLIAM SHAKESPEARE

10

What is past my help
is past my care.
JOHN FLETCHER

11

Let us have wine and women,
mirth and laughter,
Sermons and soda-water
the day after.
LORD BYRON

12

Truth lies within a little
and certain compass,
but error is immense.
VISCOUNT BOLINGBROKE

13

A man hath no better thing under
the sun, than to eat, and to drink,
and to be merry.
THE BIBLE. ECCLESIASTES

14

Those have most power to hurt us,
that we love.
FRANCIS BEAUMONT

15

But what is freedom?
Rightly understood,
A universal license to be good.
HARTLEY COLERIDGE

16

Small habits, well pursued betimes,
May reach the dignity of crimes.
HANNAH MORE

17

A sorrow's crown of sorrow
is remembering happier things.
ALFRED, LORD TENNYSON

18

Business first;
pleasure afterwards.
WILLIAM MAKEPEACE THACKERAY

19

The way to ensure summer in England
is to have it framed and glazed in
a comfortable room.
HORACE WALPOLE
4th EARL OF ORFORD

20

He jests at scars
that never felt a wound.
WILLIAM SHAKESPEARE

Serene I fold my hands and wait,
Nor care for wind, nor tide, nor sea;
I rave no more 'gainst time or fate,
For lo! my own shall come to me.
JOHN BURROUGHS

21

Nothing is so useless
as a general maxim.
LORD MACAULAY

22

Philosophy will clip
an angel's wings.
JOHN KEATS

23

Absence of occupation is not rest,
A mind quite vacant,
is a mind distressed.
WILLIAM COWPER

24

Lukewarmness I count a sin
As great in love as in religion.
ABRAHAM COWLEY

25

If you would hit the mark, you must
aim a little above it;
Every arrow that flies feels the·
attraction of earth.
HENRY WADSWORTH LONGFELLOW

26

'Tis not the drinking
that is to be blamed,
but the excess.
JOHN SELDEN

27

Opinion is ultimately determined
by the feelings, and not
by the intellect.
HERBERT SPENCER

28

Live as long as you may, the first
twenty years are the longest half
of your life.
ROBERT SOUTHEY

29

There is no duty we so much
underrate as the duty
of being happy.
ROBERT LOUIS STEVENSON

30

But words are words;
I never yet did hear
That the bruised heart was pierced
through the ear.
WILLIAM SHAKESPEARE

JULY

The sleep flower sways in the wheat its head,
Heavy with dreams, as that with bread:
The goodly grain and the sun-flushed sleeper
The reaper reaps, and Time the reaper.

FRANCIS THOMPSON

1

If the first of July
it be rainy weather,
'twill rain more or less
for four weeks together.
THOMAS FULLER

2

Wise men have their mouth
in their heart, fools their heart
in their mouth.
BRATHWAIT

3

There is more pleasure in loving
than in being beloved.
THOMAS FULLER

4

The robb'd that smiles
steals something from the thief.
WILLIAM SHAKESPEARE

5

There was never yet philosopher
That could endure the toothache
patiently.
WILLIAM SHAKESPEARE

6

Laughter is not at all a bad
beginning for a friendship, and it
is far the best ending for one.
OSCAR WILDE

7

Do not miss what is near
by aiming at what is afar.
EURIPIDES

8

Bachelor's fare:
bread and cheese and kisses.
JONATHAN SWIFT

Ah, make the most of what we yet may spend
Before we too into the Dust descend:
Dust into Dust, and under Dust, to lie,
Sans Wine, sans Song, sans Singer, and — sans end.
OMAR KHAYYAM. FIRST EDITION 1859

9

Comfort. n.
A state of mind produced by
contemplation of a
neighbour's uneasiness.
AMBROSE BIERCE

10

He is a first rate collector
who can, upon all occasions
collect his wits.
GEORGE DENNISON PRENTICE

11

Love is Nature's second son.
GEORGE CHAPMAN

12

Good friends, good books and a
sleepy conscience:
this is the ideal life.
MARK TWAIN

13

Sleep, riches, and health,
to be truly enjoyed,
must be interrupted.
JEAN PAUL RICHTER

14

Old friends are best.
King James used to call for
his old shoes; they were
easiest for his feet.
JOHN SELDEN

15

There are three things which
the public will always clamour for,
sooner or later:
namely, Novelty, novelty, novelty.
THOMAS HOOD

16

Scenery is fine —
but human nature is finer.
JOHN KEATS

17

Wagner has lovely moments
but awful quarters of an hour.
GIOACCHINO ROSSINI

18

How often misused words
generate misleading thoughts.
HERBERT SPENCER

19

The truth is rarely pure
and never simple.
OSCAR WILDE

20

No man is exempt from saying
silly things; the mischief is
to say them deliberately.
MONTAIGNE

> When at last they rose to go to bed,
> it struck each man as he followed
> his neighbour upstairs,
> that the one before him walked
> very crookedly.
> ROBERT SMITH SURTEES

21

A wise woman never
yields by appointment.
STENDHAL

22

We think caged birds sing
when indeed they cry.
JOHN WEBSTER

23

Beware of all enterprises
that require new clothes.
THOREAU

24

When will the world know that
peace and procreation are the two
most delightful things in it.
HORACE WALPOLE

25

There is a charm about the
forbidden that makes it
unspeakably desirable.
MARK TWAIN

26

Orthodoxy is my doxy;
heterodoxy is another man's doxy.
BISHOP WILLIAM WARBURTON

27

And when you stick on
     conversation's burrs,
Don't strew your pathway
     with those dreadful 'urs'
OLIVER WENDELL HOLMES

28

They never taste who always drink;
They always talk, who never think.
MATTHEW PRIOR

29

To be totally understanding
makes one very indulgent.
MADAM DE STAEL

30

Satire is a sort of glass
wherein beholders do generally
discover everybody's face
but their own.
JONATHAN SWIFT

31

Proportion is almost impossible to
human beings. There is no one who
does not exaggerate.
EMERSON

AUGUST

Wou'd you gain the tender creature?
Softly, gently, kindly treat her,
Suffering is the lover's part.
Beauty by constraint possessing
You enjoy but half the blessing,
lifeless charms without the heart.

JOHN GAY

1

To love oneself is the beginning of
a life-long romance.
OSCAR WILDE

2

Sincerity is the highest compliment
you can pay.
EMERSON

3

Two things doth prolong thy life:
a quiet heart and a loving wife.
THOMAS DELONEY

4

True love is like ghosts,
which everybody talks about
and few have seen.
LA ROCHEFOUCAULD

5

. . . because I love you,
I would sooner have you hate me for
telling you the truth
than adore me for telling you lies.
PIETRO ARETINO

6

The instinct of man
is to pursue the things
that fly from him, and fly
from the things which pursue him.
VOLTAIRE

7

It is very foolish to wish
to be exclusively wise.
LA ROCHEFOUCAULD

8

Our safety is not in blindness,
but in facing our dangers.
SCHOPENHAUER

One Moment in Annihilation's Waste,
One Moment, of the Well of Life to taste —
The Stars are setting and the Caravan
Starts for the Dawn of Nothing — Oh, make haste
OMAR KHAYYAM. FIRST EDITION 1859

9

No man was ever great
by imitation.
SAMUEL JOHNSON

10

Great blunders are often made,
like large ropes,
of a multitude of fibres.
VICTOR HUGO

11

True disputants
are like true sportsmen:
their whole delight is
in the dispute.
ALEXANDER POPE

12

Those who make the
worst use of their time
are the first to complain
of its brevity.
LA BRUYERE

13

It is only when the rich
are sick that they fully feel
the impotence of wealth.
CHARLES CALEB COLTON

14

A metaphysician:
a blind man in a dark room –
looking for a black hat –
which isn't there.
CHARLES BROWN

15

Winter's thunder and summer's flood
Never boded Englishman good.
JOHN RAY

16

A man is as old as he's feeling
a woman as old as she looks.
MORTIMER COLLINS

17

Vanity, like murder, will out.
HANNAH COWLEY

18

The only way to get rid
of temptation
is to yield to it.
OSCAR WILDE

19

What is a communist?
One who has yearnings
For equal divisions of
unequal earnings.
EBENEZER ELLIOT

20

An open foe may prove a curse,
But a pretended friend is worse.
JOHN GAY

Here with a loaf of bread beneath the bough
A Flask of Wine, a Book of Verse — and Thou
Beside me singing in the Wilderness —
And Wilderness is Paradise Enow.
OMAR KHAYYAM. FIRST EDITION 1859

21

Love is a circle
that doth restless move
In the same sweet eternity of love.
ROBERT HERRICK

22

One should never put on one's
best trousers to go out to battle
for freedom and truth.
HENRIK IBSEN

23

It is one thing to show a man that
he is in an error, and another to
put him in possession of truth.
JOHN LOCKE

24

If the twenty fourth of August
be fair and clear, then hope for a
prosperous Autumn that year.
THOMAS FULLER

25

Art is long, and Time is fleeting.
HENRY WADSWORTH LONGFELLOW

26

Be wisely worldly,
be not worldly wise.
FRANCIS QUARLES

27

In all pleasure hope is a
considerable part.
SAMUEL JOHNSON

28

As is our confidence,
so is our capacity.
WILLIAM HAZLITT

29

The grandeur of man stems
from his knowledge of his own
misery. A tree does not know
itself to be miserable.
PASCAL

30

It is not irregular hours or
irregular diet that make the
romantic life.
EMERSON

31

A fool is only troublesome,
a pedant unsupportable.
NAPOLEON I

SEPTEMBER

'I saw you take his kiss!' ''Tis true.'
'O modesty!' ''Twas strictly kept:
He thought me asleep; at least, I knew
He thought I thought he thought I slept.'
COVENTRY PATMORE

1

To be angry is to revenge
the fault of others upon ourselves.
ALEXANDER POPE

2

He who is in love with himself
has at least this advantage —
He won't encounter many rivals.
GEORG LICHTENBERG

3

Sobriety is the love of health,
or the inability to eat.
LA ROCHEFOUCAULD

4

The virtue which requires
to be ever guarded
is scarce worth the sentinel.
OLIVER GOLDSMITH

5

The old believe everything,
the middle-aged suspect everything,
the young know everything.
OSCAR WILDE

6

One word frees us of all
the weight and pain of life:
that word is love.
SOPHOCLES

7

I have never known any
distress that an hour's reading
did not alleviate.
MONTESQUIEU

8

Every advantage has its tax.
EMERSON

Ah Love, could Thou and I with Fate conspire
To grasp this sorry Scheme of Things entire,
    Would we not shatter it to bits — and then
Remould it nearer to the Heart's Desire!
OMAR KHAYYAM. FIRST EDITION 1859

9

Absence sharpens love,
presence strengthens it.
THOMAS FULLER

10

The discovery of a new dish
does more for the
happiness of mankind than the
discovery of a star.
BRILLAT SAVARIN

11

Nothing is more difficult,
and therefore more precious than
to be able to decide.
NAPOLEON I

12

Hope is the only good thing
that disillusion respects.
VAUVENARGUES

13

No man can be happy
without a friend,
nor be sure of his friend
till he is unhappy.
THOMAS FULLER

14

Exuberance is beauty.
GUSTAVE FLAUBERT

15

Indolence is a delightful
but distressing state:
we must be doing something
to be happy.
WILLIAM HAZLITT

16

Memory is the diary that
we all carry about with us.
OSCAR WILDE

17

The longer we live,
the more we find we are
like other people.
OLIVER WENDELL HOLMES

18

He who is by nature
not his own but another's man,
is by nature a slave.
ARISTOTLE

19

Dare to be true
nothing can need a lie;
a fault which needs it most
grows therebye.
GEORGE HERBERT

20

Diffidence is the
better part of knowledge.
CHARLES CALEB COLTON

No human being, however great or powerful
was ever as free as a fish
JOHN RUSKIN

21

I must have women.
There is nothing unbends
the mind like them.
JOHN GAY

22

He was so generally civil,
that nobody thanked him for it.
SAMUEL JOHNSON

23

The greatest pleasure I know,
is to do a good action by stealth,
and to have it found out
by accident.
CHARLES LAMB

24

Think nothing done
while aught remains to do.
SAMUEL ROGERS

25

Poets are the unacknowledged
legislators of the world.
PERCY BYSSHE SHELLEY

26

The quarrels of lovers
are the renewals of love.
TERENCE

27

Make hunger thy sauce,
as a medicine for health.
THOMAS TUSSER

28

It is the heretic
that makes the fire,
Not she which burns in 't.
WILLIAM SHAKESPEARE

29

'Tis safest in matrimony to begin
with a little aversion.
RICHARD BRINSLEY SHERIDAN

30

An elegant sufficiency, content,
retirement, rural quiet,
friendship, books.
JAMES THOMSON

OCTOBER

There is no excellent beauty
that hath not some strangeness
in the proportion.
FRANCIS BACON

1

Superstition sets
the entire world in flames.
Philosophy puts them out.
VOLTAIRE

2

Why care for grammar
as long as we are good.
ARTEMUS WARD

3

Of all axioms this
shall win the prize —
'Tis better to be fortunate
than wise.
JOHN WEBSTER

4

An ambassador is an honest man,
sent to lie abroad
for the good of his country.
SIR HENRY WOTTON

5

There ain't no way to find out
why a snorer can't
hear himself snore.
MARK TWAIN

6

Genius does what it must,
and talent does what it can.
OWEN MEREDITH

7

Experience joined
with common sense,
To mortals is a providence.
MATTHEW GREEN

8

Invention breeds invention.
EMERSON

If youth is a season of hope, it is often so
only in the sense that our elders
are hopeful about us: for no age is so apt
to think its emotions are
the last of their kind.
GEORGE ELIOT

9

Beauty is a lover's gift.
WILLIAM CONGREVE

10

Truth is the cry of all,
but the game of the few.
BISHOP BERKELEY

11

Life is the art of drawing
sufficient conclusions from
insufficient premises.
SAMUEL BUTLER

12

One of the greatest pleasures
of life is conversation.
SYDNEY SMITH

13

If you wait on tomorrow
you will miss today.
ENGLISH PROVERB

14

A word in season is most precious.
AESOP

15

How eternally amused one is
at the convictions
of one's neighbours — imperturbably
admitting reciprocity.
OLIVER WENDELL HOLMES

16

Ideas often flash across our minds
more complete than we could make
them after great labour.
LA ROCHEFOUCAULD

17

I always like to have the morning
well-aired before I get up.
BEAU BRUMMELL

18

Necessity does the work of courage.
GEORGE ELIOT

19

The saying that beauty is skin deep
is but a skin deep saying.
JOHN RUSKIN

20

Men, like peaches and pears,
grow sweet a little while before
they begin to decay.
OLIVER WENDELL HOLMES

Love reckons hours for months,
and days for years;
And every little absence is an age.
JOHN DRYDEN

21

Music revives the recollections
it would appease.
MADAME DE STAEL

22

People who have no weaknesses
are terrible; there is no way
of taking advantage of them.
ANATOLE FRANCE

23

They who prosper
take on airs of vanity.
AESCHYLUS

24

Deliberation. n.
The act of examining one's bread
to determine which side
it is buttered on.
AMBROSE BIERCE

25

How strangely we diminish
a thing as soon as we try to
express it in words.
MAETERLINCK

26

Work is not the curse,
but drudgery is.
HENRY WARD BEECHER

27

Nothing can be so perfect
when we possess it as it will
seem when remembered.
OLIVER WENDELL HOLMES

28

Can love be controll'd by advice'
JOHN GAY

29

Whoever would lie usefully
should lie seldom.
LORD HERVEY

30

Cynicism is intellectual dandyism.
GEORGE MEREDITH

31

Rulers have no authority
from God to do mischief.
JONATHAN MAYHEW

NOVEMBER

I saw old Autumn in the misty morn
Stand shadowless like Silence, listening
To silence.

THOMAS HOOD

1

The secret of being boring is —
say everything.
VOLTAIRE

2

Why has not man a microscopic eye?
For this plain reason,
man is not a fly.
ALEXANDER POPE

3

Architecture in general
is frozen music.
FRIEDRICH VON SCHELLING

4

Everyone lives by
selling something.
ROBERT LOUIS STEVENSON

5

It is because we put up with
bad things that hotel keepers
continue to give them to us.
ANTHONY TROLLOPE

6

It is better to wear out
than rust out.
BISHOP RICHARD CUMBERLAND

7

Do not adultery commit;
Advantage rarely comes of it.
ARTHUR HUGH CLOUGH

8

If you tell the truth you don't
have to remember anything.
MARK TWAIN

In itself and in its consequences the life
of leisure is beautiful and ennobling
in all civilised men's eyes
THORSTEIN VEBLEN

9

Modesty is the only sure
bait when you angle for praise.
LORD CHESTERFIELD

10

Meekness. n.
Uncommon patience in planning
a revenge that is worth while.
AMBROSE BIERCE

11

Clothes and manners do not make
the man, but, when he is made, they
greatly improve his appearance.
HENRY WARD BEECHER

12

Look for the ridiculous in
everything and you will find it.
JULES RENARD

13

A single conversation across
the table with a wise man is
better than ten years'
mere study of books.
LONGFELLOW

14

Experience is a comb
which nature gives us
when we are bald.
CHINESE PROVERB

15

When a man does not write his
poetry, it escapes by
other vents through him.
EMERSON

16

Is it not strange that desire
should so many years
,outlive performance.
WILLIAM SHAKESPEARE

17

Pleasure's a sin, and sometimes
sin's a pleasure.
LORD BYRON

18

If a man sits down to think,
he is immediately asked
if he has the headache.
EMERSON

19

We often get in quicker by the back
door than the front.
NAPOLEON I

20

A good edge is good for nothing
if it has nothing to cut.
THOMAS FULLER

It is very strange and very melancholy,
that the paucity of human pleasures
should persuade us ever to call
hunting one of them.
SAMUEL JOHNSON

21

The young suffer less from
their own errors than from
the cautiousness of the old.
VAUVENARGUES

22

The present time has
one advantage over every other –
it is our own.
CHARLES CALEB COLTON

23

Evidence of trust begets trust.
PLUTARCH

24

Love is reciprocated by love.
PLUTARCH

25

Life is a joke that's just begun.
W. S. GILBERT

26

We are all Adam's children
but silk makes the difference.
THOMAS FULLER

27

Experience teaches slowly
and at the cost of mistakes.
J. A. FROUDE

28

Death, in itself, is nothing;
but we fear,
To be we know not what,
we know not where.
JOHN DRYDEN

29

The Youth of a Nation
are the trustees of Posterity.
BENJAMIN DISRAELI

30

A joke's a very serious thing.
CHARLES CHURCHILL

DECEMBER

The trumpet of prophecy! O, Wind,
If Winter comes, can Spring be far behind?
PERCY BYSSHE SHELLEY

1

I do not mind lying,
but I hate inaccuracy.
SAMUEL BUTLER

2

You can never plan the
future by the past.
EDMUND BURKE

3

Love and scandal are the
best sweeteners of tea.
HENRY FIELDING

4

Pure and complete sorrow is
as impossible as
pure and complete joy.
LEO TOLSTOY

5

Cowardly dogs bark loudest.
JOHN WEBSTER

6

Nature is very consonant
and comfortable with herself.
SIR ISAAC NEWTON

7

I can never feel certain
of any truth
but from a clear perception
of its beauty.
JOHN KEATS

8

Talking and eloquence are
not the same:
to speak, and speak well,
are two things.
BEN JONSON

No man who has ever heartily and wholly laughed
can be altogether irreclaimably bad.
THOMAS CARLYLE

9

If suffer we must,
let's suffer on the heights.
VICTOR HUGO

10

Mix some foolishness
with serious plans,
it is pleasant to be silly
at the right moment.
HORACE

11

Anger is never without
an argument, but seldom
with a good one.
GEORGE SAVILE

12

Malice is of low stature,
but it hath very long arms.
GEORGE SAVILE

13

The superiority of one man's
opinion over another's is
never so great as when
the opinion is about a woman.
HENRY JAMES

14

If you are idle,
be not solitary;
if you are solitary,
be not idle.
SAMUEL JOHNSON

15

Ill news hath wings,
and with the wind doth go,
Comfort's a cripple,
and comes ever slow.
MICHAEL DRAYTON

16

No one ever became
depraved suddenly.
JUVENAL

17

A wise scepticism is the first
attribute of a good critic.
JAMES RUSSELL LOWELL

18

I expect that Woman will be
the last thing civilised by Man.
GEORGE MEREDITH

19

Virtue, in the great world,
should be amenable.
MOLIERE

20

Great lords have their pleasures,
but people have fun.
MONTESQUIEU

Our minds need relaxation, and give way
Unless we mix with work a little play.
MOLIERE

21

For each age is a dream
that is dying,
Or one that is coming to birth.
ARTHUR O'SHAUGHNESSY

22

Taxation without representation
is tyranny.
JAMES OTIS

23

The heart has its own reasons
which reason knows nothing of.
BLAISE PASCAL

24

Go, teach eternal wisdom
how to rule —
Then drop into thyself,
and be a fool!
ALEXANDER POPE

25

Every man loves what he is good at.
THOMAS SHADWELL

26

Even as they teach, men learn.
SENECA

27

A good book is the best of friends,
the same today and for ever.
MARTIN TUPPER

28

Take my word for it,
the silliest woman in the world
can manage a clever man;
but it takes a very clever woman
to manage a fool.
RUDYARD KIPLING

29

Passion, though a bad regulator,
is a powerful spring.
EMERSON

30

The most positive men are
the most credulous.
ALEXANDER POPE

31

Kissing don't last:
cookery do!
GEORGE MEREDITH

Text compilation copyright © 1981 Suzy Siddons
Colour illustrations copyright Mrs M G Anderson

ISBN 0 340 27455 7

First published 1981
Second impression 1982

Published by Hodder and Stoughton Children's Books,
a division of Hodder and Stoughton Ltd,
Mill Road, Dunton Green, Sevenoaks, Kent TN13 2YJ.

Compiled by Suzy Siddons
Designed by Mark Gerlings
Decorative initials by Charlotte Gerlings
Origination by Anglia Reproductions Ltd, Witham, Essex.
Printed in Great Britain by Waterlow Limited, Dunstable